Charles H. Possons

Resources and Attractions of Hoosick Falls, N.Y.

Its location, surroundings

Charles H. Possons

Resources and Attractions of Hoosick Falls, N.Y.
Its location, surroundings

ISBN/EAN: 9783337193454

Printed in Europe, USA, Canada, Australia, Japan

Cover: Foto ©Andreas Hilbeck / pixelio.de

More available books at **www.hansebooks.com**

THE FALLS.

RESOURCES AND ATTRACTIONS

of

HOOSICK FALLS, N. Y.

Its

Location, Surroundings, Water Power, Railroad Facilities, Schools, Churches, Industries, Institutions, Etc., Etc.

1890

Published for the Hoosick Falls Board of Trade

INTRODUCTORY.

THIS publication is issued under the auspices of the Hoosick Falls Board of Trade, which consists of the leading and active business and professional men of the village. The object of the association is to promote the prosperity of Hoosick Falls; to collect and disseminate information and facts that shall tend to induce new enterprises to locate here; to encourage enterprises already started; to encourage intercourse between business men; to endeavor by all proper means to attract to the village such capital business enterprises, inventions, and manufactories as shall promote its growth; and by systematic, careful and judicious methods contribute to the advancement of the general interests of the whole community. In this work we have sought to present, in an unprejudiced manner, the general attractions of Hoosick Falls from many standpoints, our aim being not to attract manufacturers only, but good citizens of all classes. Hoosick Falls possesses important natural advantages; it is progressive and enterprising and the Board of Trade stands ready to do anything that may assist in increasing its industrial resources.

HOOSICK · FALLS · BOARD · OF · TRADE

OFFICERS.

W. M. HOLMES,	*President*
JOS. BUCKLEY,	*First Vice-President*
FRANK RILEY,	*Second Vice-President*
C. Q. ELDREDGE,	*Secretary*
E. M. JONES,	*Treasurer*

EXECUTIVE COMMITTEE.

W. M. HOLMES,
JOS. BUCKLEY,
FRANK RILEY,
C. Q. ELDREDGE,
E. M. JONES,
JOSEPH HAUSSLER,
EDGAR LEONARD,
A. L. JOHNSON,
J. G. BYARS, SR.,
BENJ. HORSLEY.

STANDING COMMITTEES.

ON MEMBERSHIP

JOSEPH HAUSSLER, H. W. STONE, JOHN GIBSON.

ON FINANCE.

EDGAR LEONARD, PETER GAFFNEY, C. D. KINSLEY.

ON TRADE AND MANUFACTURES.

A. L. JOHNSTON, W. G. PARSONS, WM. SHERIDAN, A. C. LOTTRIDGE, L. E. WORDEN.

ON PUBLIC WORKS.

J. G. BYARS, SR., C. W. EASTON, JOHN DOLIN.

ON STATISTICS.

BENJ. HORSLEY, GEO. E. GREENE, NELSON GILLESPIE.

MEMBERS.

Archibald, W. M. . . . . Drugs
Baker, Fred. E. . . . . Clerk
Barnes, Horace H. . . . . Foreman W. A. Wood M. & R. M. Co.
Berger, H. P. (H. P. Berger & Co.) . . . . Furniture
Blanshfield, Wm. . . . . Grocer
Brackman & Levy . . . . Clothing
Brien Bros. . . . . Hardware
Buckley, Jos. . . . . Grocer, Coal and Wood
Byars, James G. . . . . Bottler
Cheney, C. A. . . Chief Accountant W. A. Wood M. & R. M. Co.
Clark, Byron F. . . . . Grocer
Copeland, W. H. . Ass't Ch'f Acct'nt W. A. Wood M. & R. M. Co.
Covey, A. B. . . . . Livery
Darling, David . . . . Builder
Darroch, John G. . . . . Stoves, etc.
DeLong B. F. . . . . Meat Market
Dolin, John . . . . Brick
Easton, C. W. (Easton, Rising & Worden) . . Lumber, Coal, etc.
Eldredge, Chas. Q. Real Estate
Eldredge, J. Wm. . . . . Clerk
Ely, W. H. (Wallace, Jones & Ely) . . . . General Store
Fitch, F. S., Jr. . . . . Dry Goods
Gaffney, Peter (Riley & Gaffney) . . . . Livery, Coal, etc.
Geer, Danforth . . . . Ass't Sec'y W. A Wood M. & R. M. Co.
Gibson, John . . . . Wall Paper
Gillespie, Nelson (Gillespie Bros.) . . . . Dry Goods
Greene, George E. . . . . Attorney
Halsey, A. C. . . . . Hotel
Hammond, F. S. . . . . Manager Co-operative Store
Haren, P. J. . . . . Hotel
Harrington, A. B. . . . . Editor Hoosick Valley *Democrat*
Haussler, Joseph . . . . Postmaster
Hayfield, T. H. . . . . Billiard Parlor
Healy, M. C. . . . . Hotel
Heaton, Willis E. . . . . Attorney
Holmes, H. A. . . . . Inventor
Holmes, W. M. . . . . Inventor
Horsley, Benj. . . . . . Proprietor Rensselaer County *Standard*
Hudson, F. R. . . . . Physician
Hurd, E. B. . . . . Lumber, Coal, Hardware, etc.
Hyland, William . . . . Grocer
Johnson, D. C. . . . . Clerk
Johnston, A. L. General Merchant
Jones, E. M. (Wallace, Jones & Ely) . . . . General Store
Jones, Ernest C. (Gibson & Jones) . . . . Grocer
Joslin, Geo. W. . . . . Baker
Kegler, A. G. . . . . Clerk
Kimpner, Sol. S. . . . . Restaurant
Kincaid, M. D. . . . . Clothing

Kinsley, C. D. . . . . Attorney
Lasor, Charles . . . Painter, and Manager Wood's Opera House
Leonard, Edgar . . . . Express and Ice
Levy, Edward . . . . Manager Rochester Clothing Store
Lottridge, A. C. Builder, etc.
Lurie, P. . . . . Dry Goods
March, C. B. . . . . Clerk
Markstone, Louis . . . . Boots and Shoes
McEachron, J. H. (McEachron & Robson) . . . . Jeweler
McKearin, P. . . . . Manager Western Union Telegraph Office
Miller, J. M. . . . . Merchant
Murphy, Martin . . . . Meat Market
Murray, John . . . . Grocer
Nichols, Geo. H., Jr. . Purchasing Agt. W. A. Wood M. & R. M. Co.
Nichols, W. S. . . . Vice-President W. A. Wood M. & R. M. Co.
Otey, John . . . .
Parsons, Hinsdill . . . . Patent Attorney
Parsons, Willard P. . . . . Civil Engineer
Parsons, J. Russell . . . . Attorney W. A. Wood M. & R. M. Co.
Parsons, Warren G. . . . . Merchant
Pincus & Abram . . . . Clothing
Platto, C. V. L. . . . . Correspondent
Putnam, W. B. . . . . Physician
Redmond, J. J. . . . . Grocer
Riley, Frank (Riley & Gaffney) . . . . Livery, Coal, etc.
Riley, Hugh A. (Watrous & Riley) . . . . Hardware
Rising, C. F. (Easton, Rising & Worden) Lumber, Hardware, etc.
Robson, C. A. (McEachron & Robson) . . . . Jeweler
Runkle, D. . . . . Collection Dept. W. A. Wood M. & R. M. Co.
Sawyer, John T. . . . . Manager Electric Light Co.
Sheridan, William . . . . Wines and Liquors
Shull, John E. . . . . Superintendent of Schools
Sipperly, John A. . . . . Photographer
Slocum, A. J. . . . . Grocer
Smith, C. F. W. . . . . Druggist
Spencer, Chas. C. . . . . Foreman W. A. Wood M. & R. M. Co.
Stevens, Frank L. . . . Supt. Stevens & Thompson Paper Mills
Stevens, S. S. (Stevens & Thompson) . . . . Paper Mills
Stone, Henry W. Druggist
Thorpe, Geo. E. . . . . Druggist
Van Hyning, Geo. W. . . . . Clothing
Waddell, James . . . . Tailor
Watrous, E. G. . . . . Inventor
White, Frank H. . . . . Meat Market
White, Salem H. . . . . Meat Market
Wilder, Lyman C. . . . . Real Estate
Wood, W. A. . . . . Pres't W. A. Wood M. & R. M. Co.
Worden, L. E. (Easton, Rising & Worden), Lumber, Hardware, etc.
Youlen, P. M. . . . . Watchmaker and Jeweler

QUESTIONS

BY THE

Hoosick Falls Board of Trade.

Do you know that Hoosick Falls has an undeveloped water-power aggregating nearly 2000 horse-power?

Do you know that Hoosick Falls has many desirable sites for manufacturing establishments?

Do you know that Hoosick Falls has good railroad facilities with through trains to Boston, New York, Chicago, St. Louis, and Montreal?

Do you know that Hoosick Falls gives employment to nearly 3000 of her citizens in her manufactories?

Do you know that the population of Hoosick Falls is rapidly increasing?

Do you know that Hoosick Falls has a complete system of water works with a never-failing supply of pure water; and that the power which forces it through the entire village is sufficient to throw it over the highest buildings?

Do you know that Hoosick Falls has gas works, electric lights, two newspapers, a solid bank, and a perfect telephone service?

Do you know that Hoosick Falls has a fire department to be proud of?

Do you know that Hoosick Falls has five churches of as many denominations?

Do you know that Hoosick Falls has a prosperous Young Men's Christian Association?

Do you know that Hoosick Falls has a system of public schools second to no other place of comparative size in the State?

VIEW ON MAIN STREET

Residence of Hon. Walter A. Wood.

Residence and Office of Chas. Q. Eldredge.

Do you know that Hoosick Falls has the Citizens' Corps, one of the finest military organizations in the State; and a State Armory which cost $40,000?

Do you know that Hoosick Falls has a Grand Army Post, lodges of various orders, and prominent social clubs?

Do you know that Hoosick Falls is in the midst of a rich agricultural region, and is surrounded by scenery of surpassing loveliness?

Do you know that Hoosick Falls has two Building and Loan Associations, which build houses for their members?

Do you know that the laboring people of Hoosick Falls generally own their own homes?

Do you know that new-comers to Hoosick Falls will have the advantage of all completed improvements, and will not have to pay for them as they would in a new town?

Do you know that Hoosick Falls has a Board of Trade made up of about one hundred of her best business men, who are working together to increase the importance of the village?

Do you know that taxes are low in Hoosick Falls?

Do you know that your best interests dictate that you visit Hoosick Falls or correspond with the Board of Trade before locating elsewhere?

As the Board of Trade *does know* that the facts suggested by the above questions are true, it cordially commends Hoosick Falls as a residence, and a desirable point for business and manufacturing.

THE PAST.

IT IS not to be expected that in a work of this kind, necessarily compact and brief in character, the compiler should enter into a detailed and particular account of historical events, consequently much that is of itself interesting must be entirely ignored, the seeker for mere literary amusement being referred to purely historical publications.

The word Hoosick is of Aboriginal derivation. Judge Ball, the historian of the section, says the meaning of the word is "stony place," and that it is derived from the two Indian words *Hussen* and *ack* or *ick*. The spelling of the word, as adopted by the United States Government, is as written above. Beyond the border, in Massachusetts, however, the same river here called Hoosick is written "Hoosac," and the latter spelling is applied to the range of mountains pierced by the famous Hoosac Tunnel. In opposition to Judge Ball another writer of history evolves from the word, "Owl Valley," or "Valley of the Owl," *Hoo* being the Indian name for owl, and *sac* for valley. The application of either writer is good. Certainly the vicinity of the Hoosac Mountains is a "stony place," while the beautiful valley in the vicinity of Hoosick Falls is fair to look upon, and gives rise to the question "*Hoo* would not be glad to have it for a home?"

The township of Hoosick embraces about 38,000 acres. The township of Hoosick was formed March 24, 1772. Within the town, a little more than five years later, was fought one of the most decisive battles of the Revolution —the first check to the triumphant Burgoyne. But for the victory here achieved England would no doubt have conquered the colonists. Indeed, the event, which has ever been conceded to be decisive of American liberty on this continent, decided the course of France in espousing the cause of the colonies, and thus assured the Independence of America. We refer to the so-called Battle of Bennington. True, the English expedition designed capturing stores at Bennington, but, nevertheless, the battle was fought in the town of Hoosick, but a short distance from Hoosick Falls, near the Walloomsac River, and should properly be called *Battle of Walloomsac*. The story of the battle has often been told. August 16, 1777, Gen. John Stark, of New Hampshire, commanding a hastily-gathered force of militia, defeated a detachment of Gen. Burgoyne's army under Col. Baum. Gen. Burgoyne, with an army of invasion from Canada, was marching towards New York, expecting to form a junction with a force sent up the Hudson by Howe, the British commander there, at or near Albany. The object of these movements was to cut off New England from the rest of the country. Burgoyne's march from Canada had been one of triumph, very much like that of a conqueror. Becoming short of provisions, and knowing that considerable stores were collected at Bennington as a depot for the American army, Burgoyne resolved to seize it for the use of his own forces. He selected for that purpose a force of German regulars, some Canadians, a corps of provincials (tories), and over 100 Indians, with two pieces of artillery. This force was completely routed by Gen. Stark. The loss to the Americans was thirty killed and forty wounded; that of the English, two pieces of brass cannon, seven hundred stand of arms, seven hundred prisoners, two hundred and seven dead on the spot, and a large number of wounded. The injury to the enemy by this disaster can scarcely be estimated. It was not confined to loss of men and munitions of war. The victory was the first check given to the march of Burgoyne. By its depressing effect on the spirits of the enemy, and the confidence in their powers with which it inspired the Americans, the current of success was at once turned from the British to the American arms.

The first settlement of Hoosick Falls was about the time of the formation of the township, in 1772. A few years later the water-power of the cataract here began to be utilized, and extensive carding, fulling and cloth-dressing works were built, followed by a grist-mill, saw-mill and flax-mill, and a distillery. Still later large cotton-mills were operated here, continuing until about 1840.

Hoosick Falls was incorporated as a village in 1827. The population was then 200, the houses, 36, the voters, 50, the valuation, $96,370, and the length of the streets less than two miles.

Having indulged in history to this extent let us now take up Hoosick Falls as we find it to-day, hoping that he who reads what may be said of the village will be interested therein, and become imbued with a desire to know more about it.

VIEW ON CHURCH STREET.

HOOSICK FALLS.

HOOSICK FALLS is a very attractive village of nearly 8000 inhabitants, charmingly located on the Hoosick River. The physical features of the township are marked by ranges of hills cut by fertile valleys, through which the Hoosick River and the Walloomsac River flow. To the east is the Taghanic range of mountains, while on the west is the Petersburgh range. Indeed, the mountains and hills are a permanent feature of the landscape. Nowhere in this vicinity is the sight of them or the inspiring sense of their presence altogether wanting.

The town is divided into two nearly equal parts by the Hoosick River. This is a historic stream, whose valley was the war-path along which the French and Indians made their stealthy marches upon the villages of New England. The Walloomsac River empties into the Hoosick a short distance from Hoosick Falls. Both of these streams are rapid and their waters turn the wheels of many busy factories. The Hoosick winds through the village in the shape of a letter "S." Above the falls excellent facilities for boating are presented, and this form of recreation is much enjoyed by many of the villagers.

Hoosick Falls is situated on the great Fitchburg Railroad, 163 miles from Boston, 27 miles from Troy, 32 miles from Albany, and 182 miles from New York. The ride here from Boston is but five and one-half hours; from New York, five hours. Through trains run from here to Boston, New York, Chicago and Montreal.

Hoosick Falls presents all the elements of a thrifty and enterprising village. Its people have made good use of natural advantages, and stand ready to increase its usefulness and add to its strength. Peopled by an industrious population, its progress bears evidence of a spirit that overcomes all difficulties, and in this spirit the people hold out their hands to welcome all who may read of Hoosick Falls, and who may yield to the tempting advantages the village offers as a place of industry or a village of quiet homes.

The country surrounding Hoosick Falls affords a great variety of delightful walks and drives, and presents many attractive and interesting views.

Statistics prove that Hoosick Falls is one of the most healthful places in the country. Its climate is pure and genial; the village is subject to no prevailing diseases, and its sanitary condition is well regulated by an efficient board of health.

The residence portion of the town is attractive. Hoosick Falls is a village of permanent citizens, and, better than all, a community of permanent homes and home-holders. Beside the more pretentious residences located here and there throughout the village, in an atmosphere as pure as ever floated on mountain breeze, are the homes of the workingmen. At evening when the sleeve is drawn over those strong arms, around their own fireside and amid the contentment of their own household, rest the masters and owners of these homes—not crowded tenements, the abodes of darkness and despair—but bright cottages, beset with flowers blooming under the sunlight of heaven, shaded by church spires and within the sound of school bells.

In the immediate vicinity of Hoosick Falls, and in the same township, are several small villages which help swell the volume of trade here, and are of material benefit to the village. Hoosick, three miles west, has an Episcopal and a Baptist Church, and a Parish School. North Hoosick, about a mile north, has a large paper-mill, and several other industries, and a Methodist Church. A scheme is on foot to build an electric road from Hoosick Falls to North Hoosick. A little to the east of North Hoosick is Walloomsac, with a large paper-mill. Eagle Bridge is a short distance west of Hoosick Falls. The Delaware & Hudson Railroad here forms a junction with the Fitchburg. Eagle Bridge has a memorial church.

WATER WORKS.

Hoosick Falls is supplied with pure water by the Hoosick Falls Water Supply Co. The source is a gigantic well, twenty-five feet in diameter, located on the flats above the falls. Water is pumped into the main pipes direct, and also into a storage reservoir located on one of the eminences of the village. The company has about eight miles of street mains, and it supplies the village with eighty-six fire hydrants. The average pressure is eighty pounds to the square inch. The force is sufficient to throw streams from the hydrants over the highest buildings.

CHURCHES.

The churches of Hoosick Falls number five. The buildings are substantial, and the condition of their financial affairs attest the most skillful and conservative direction. The churches are as follows: St. Mark's Episcopal, Church of the Immaculate Conception (R. C.), Presbyterian, Methodist Episcopal, First Baptist. St. Mark's Church is rich in memorial gifts. In the tower is a chime of bells and a clock, presented by J. Hobart Warren, a summer resident here, in memory of his wife. A beautiful carved oak reredos, representing the Lord's Supper, is the gift of Wm. M. Cranston, of England, in memory of his wife. A brass lecturn and oak pulpit is the gift of John G. Darroch, in memory of his wife. There are also altar brasses and stained windows in memory of persons intimately connected with the parish. The new Methodist Church and the Baptist Church also have several very handsome memorial windows.

SOCIETIES.

Hoosick Falls has a number of societies of a fraternal and beneficial character, all of which are in a prosperous condition, and fulfilling the mission for which they were intended. These organizations embrace the following:

Methodist Church
First Baptist Church
St Mark's Episcopal Church
Presbyterian Church
Catholic Church

Post Wood, G. A. R., Hoosick Falls Veteran Association, Camp Byers, Sons of Veterans, Van Rensselaer Lodge, F. & A. M., Raymond Chapter, R. A. M., United Lodge, I. O. O. F., Star Lodge, K. of P., Temple of Honor, Father Matthew T. A. B. Society, Mutual Relief Society, Emerald Beneficial Assosociation, Ancient Order of Hibernians, Irish National League, O'Connell Association, etc.

SOLDIERS' MONUMENT.

Through the efforts of the Hoosick Falls Veteran Association a beautiful monument, commemorating the lives of those who fell in the War of the Rebellion, was erected in 1878, in Monument Park, at the intersection of Classic and High Streets. The monument cost $1500. One-fifth of the amount was appropriated by the town. The balance was raised by the Association.

POST WOOD, G. A. R.

Few towns evince the interest in Grand Army matters that Hoosick Falls shows. Post Wood has a membership of about 100. The hall occupied by the post is very attractive, profusely decorated, and well worthy a visit.

THE PRESS.

The press of Hoosick Falls is able and enterprising, and faithfully mirrors the events of the day. The *Rensselaer County Standard*, Benj. Horsley, proprietor, is a Republican paper. It was established nearly nineteen years ago. Under Mr. Horsley's management it has greatly increased in usefulness, and maintains a high position among the weekly papers of the State. The *Hoosick Valley Democrat* recently entered upon its fifth volume. It is published every Wednesday by Heaton & Harrington, is a clean paper typographically, attractively made up, is enterprising, and a newsy, stirring paper.

HOOSAC CLUB.

This is a social organization which evolved from the Hoosac Wheelmen, a bicycling club, organized in 1884. In May, 1890, the organization was changed to the present title. The club, which numbers about 100 of the prominent men of the village, has elegant quarters in Holmes Block, on Classic Street. The rooms are finished with hard-wood floors, and the walls are covered with felt paper. The billiard-room is 25x35 feet, and contains a pool table and a billiard table. The drawing-room and reading-room and a cosy sitting-room are handsomely furnished; there are heavy tapestry window hangings and portieres; the walls are adorned with pictures; the parlor has its piano. There are toilet-rooms and bath-rooms. In a word, the rooms are elegant and the furniture and fittings magnificent.

BANKS.

Hoosick Falls has but one banking institution—The First National. It is noted for its sound, energetic, yet conservative management, holds a high rank among the banks of the State, and commands the entire confidence of business men and capitalists. The bank has a capital of $60,000. Its last statement shows deposits amounting to $430,620.94 ; loans and discounts, $396,427.53 ; due from approved reserve agents, $101,398.56 ; due from other National banks, $14,062.29 ; surplus and undivided profits, $61,465.51.

SCHOOLS.

The people of Hoosick Falls cheerfully and liberally supply the means necessary to maintain good schools.

It is not claimed that the educational facilities here are better than anywhere else in the world ; simply that they are, at least, equal to the best found in other villages of similar size.

The affairs of the district are administered by a Board of Education, composed of three trustees, one of whom is elected annually for the term of three years.

The community is quite particular into whose hands it commits its educational interests; and hence there are selected for this important office men who are prominent for business capacity and enterprise, executive ability, and intellectual attainments. The trusteeship has been graced by such names as Hon. Walter A. Wood, J. M. Rosebrook, Joseph Buckley, Hon. J. Russell Parsons, Dr. E. P. Alden and Ambrose Carr, the last three of whom constitute the present board.

The district owns and uses three large buildings, thoroughly furnished. In each the warming, ventilating and sanitary arrangements are constructed according to modern and approved principles.

For many years Mrs. Julia M. Dewey, a scholarly lady,

and a faithful, intelligent worker, was principal of the schools, combining the functions of teacher and superintendent. She resigned her position in 1887 and is now the popular and efficient principal of the Training School at Lowell, Mass.

Mr. John E. Shull became her successor and continued serving as principal for three years, at the expiration of which time the Board of Education, authorized by a recent statute of general application to all districts of 5000 population, and over, elected him superintendent.

An able corps of twenty-seven teachers is employed. Many have had the benefit of College, Normal School or High School training, and nearly all have had considerable experience in the school-room. Their work is done with thoroughness and intelligence, and their cöoperation with the superintendent is most earnest and cordial.

The district is subject to the visitation of the Regents of the University of the State of New York, and the classes in the preliminary and advanced branches take the Regents' examinations at stated times.

The number of pupils in attendance is over 1200, and the average daily attendance is about ninety per cent. of the enrollment.

The course of study is quite similar to that of all large and progressive villages, and covers twelve years. The aim is to conduct all work according to the methods approved by our soundest educators, be those methods ancient or modern. In all the grades special effort is made to have pupils help themselves and thus induce the

High School Building
Classic Street School
Parochial School (R.C.)
Center St. School

spirit of self-dependence, and the habit of close and continued application. In the Grammar grades are completed the common branches as well as United States History, Physiology, and Book-keeping.

The High School numbers eighty scholars, including several non-residents. Its course of study extends over three years, embracing the higher mathematics, the sciences, English History, Rhetoric, Latin, Greek and French. The last-named branch is optional and extra. Latin and Greek, one or both, are elective in place of as many science studies.

Students so desiring will be fitted specially to enter College, though the system is not intended nor conducted as a feeder to higher institutions. The aim is to do the best possible for the great majority who cannot enter College. Thorough instruction in vocal music is given in all grades by an accomplished specialist, and his work is supplemented by daily practice in every school, conducted by its teacher. The corps of teachers are fitting themselves under the personal supervision of a capable instructor, to give their schools the benefit of intelligent work in form study and drawing along the lines prescribed by the State department.

The district owns a large and well-selected library, open to the public and the pupils. It is liberally used, and the effects are plainly seen in the community and the schools.

Three years ago the free text-book system was adopted. Under its use it is found possible to have a much greater variety of authors than under the old system, when the pupils bought their own books. And the aggregate cost to the district is much less.

Boasting is out of place. Yet, the school authorities earnestly invite fair and proper comparisons, to the end that its claim to excellence may be substantiated, and that the public schools may be seen to be well serving their purpose in developing the genuine manhood and womanhood that is the ripened fruit of American civilization and American institutions.

TO MANUFACTURERS.

The right place to manufacture successfully is evidently at a point where the raw material accumulates naturally, and where, at the same time, there is cheap power and ample facilities for marketing the product. Hoosick Falls presents these conditions. Situated upon a great trunk railway line connecting the village with the great markets of the East and West, the lumber regions of the North and the coal fields of the South, together with ample water-power, insures advantages to Hoosick Falls that are of vast interest to manufacturers. Factory sites can be secured in very desirable localities. Hard and soft coal, iron, lumber, timber and other material for manufacturing purposes can be brought here cheaper than to many competing places, and the facilities for distribution are ample. The manufacturer who locates here will find everything at hand for the successful furtherance of his enterprise, and a friendly and helping hand will be offered him by every citizen of the community.

The great success attained by the Walter A. Wood Mowing and Reaping Machine Co. here is an indication of what may be done in some other branch of industrial enterprise. The reaper works employ male help exclusively. Now a community embracing an army of nearly 2000 male employes in one institution naturally offers an abundance of female help. This is true of Hoosick Falls, and the manufacturer of textile goods, or of any articles in which female operatives could be employed, can readily secure the most intelligent help by locating here. Extensive stone quarries, a valuable marble quarry, brick yards, producing the best quality of brick, and adjacent timber lands, practically places building material on the site to be built upon.

WATER POWER.

Water is the cheapest power known ; and where this power can be obtained in any considerable volume there is the place to plant industrial enterprise. Hoosick Falls presents this great desideratum. Three separate localities invite attention, and the three will furnish nearly 2000 horse-power. One, on the Hoosick, is already developed and only awaits the building of factories. The dam and race-way are shown in an engraving on another page. A desirable site for any kind of manufacturing, or an establishment of great magnitude, can here be secured, with railroad tracks to the very doors. The land is comparatively level, affording the greatest facility in building.

Two other undeveloped powers are upon the Walloomsac River. High banks permit the building of dams and the construction of extensive ponds, while the territory below the dams would afford the best possible facilities for the erection of mills.

Add to cheap power the unexcelled opportunity for securing desirable help for nearly all classes of manufacturing, and it must be admitted that Hoosick Falls possesses advantages as a manufacturing centre that are worthy of the most careful investigation.

STATE ARMORY.

The armory of the 32d Separate Co. N. G. S. N. Y. is one of the handsomest buildings in Hoosick Falls; and it is a fine home for one of the crack companies of the State militia. The building and site cost $37,000. The site was purchased by Rensselaer County at a cost of $6000, and the building was erected by the State. The company expended about $3000 in fittings and furnishings, thus making the armory and appurtenances cost $40,000. The building, which is illustrated elsewhere, is 154x75 feet in dimensions. The basement is utilized as a rifle-range. The drill-room is 120x75 feet, and is without obstruction. A gallery is across one end for spectators. There are also in the building roomy officers' quarters, reading-room, parlor, locker-room, bath-room, and a band-room for the exclusive use of a band connected with the company. The band is a separate organization entirely, of thirty pieces, under the leadership of Henry Surdam.

VIEW ON CLASSIC STREET.

Armory of 32d Company, N. G. S. N. Y.

Residence of W. B. Putnam, M. D.

The officers of the company are: Chas. W. Eddy, Captain; Frank L. Stevens, First Lieutenant; Geo. H. Walden, Second Lieutenant; F. R. Hudson, M. D., Assistant Surgeon.

BUILDING AND LOAN ASSOCIATIONS.

There are two building and loan associations in Hoosick Falls, the business of which is confined to the place, and is of much benefit to many industrious citizens in aiding them to build, purchase and pay for their own homes.

The first is known as the Hoosick Building and Loan Association, which commenced business in May, 1882. Since that date this association has loaned to members over $102,000, nearly all of which amount was invested in houses in Hoosick Falls. It has never lost a dollar and has never foreclosed a mortgage, which speaks well for the management and for the members of the association. The officers are: E. R. Estabrook, President; G. A. Willis, Vice-President; B. Horsley, Treasurer; L. C. Wilder, Secretary and Attorney.

The second association was organized in June, 1889, and is doing a very conservative, profitable and extensive business of the same nature as the first Its name is The Permanent Savings and Loan Association. The total amount of money paid to the association by its members to December 1st, 1890, was $41,515.23. The following quarterly dividends have been declared: December, 1889, two per cent.; April, 1890, three per cent.; July,

1890, four per cent.; October, 1890, three per cent. Amount of capital stock paid in, $38,370.00; total profits, $3,136.23.

The officers are as follows: President, Joseph Buckley; Vice-President, John E. Shull; Secretary, C. D. Kinsley; Treasurer, P. McKearin; Attorney, G. E. Greene.

The offices of both associations are in Wilder's building, Classic Street, and the Boards of Directors meet once a month for regular business, on the 23d and 25th respectively.

POWER AND LIGHT.

The streets of Hoosick Falls are lighted by the Thomson-Houston system of electric lights under a long contract with the Hoosick Falls Water Power and Light Co. This company began operations in the autumn of 1888. It operates both arc and incandescent systems. The company has a tract of twenty-seven acres of land, which, together with the plant for lighting, cost $100,000. The Hoosick River furnishes power. A dam 150 feet long and 12 feet high was built by the company, and a raceway giving a fall of about 18 feet conducts the water to the wheels. The dam, raceway, station, and much of the lands belonging to the company are illustrated upon another page, also the railroad passing alongside the property. The company has a minimum unused power aggregating 500 horse, which will be leased on the most favorable terms to manufacturers locating here, or the company will transmit electric-power to any locality in

Hoosick Falls that may be desired. The officers of the company are: Hon. James W. Wakefield, President; Frank A. Sawyer, Treasurer; John T. Sawyer, Secretary and Manager. The company is progressive and liberal. It has been built up through the earnest efforts of Mr. John T. Sawyer, its efficient manager, to whom much credit is due for the fine plant and the development of the excellent water-power, which, we believe, will in the near future prove of vast benefit to Hoosick Falls.

MANUFACTURING.

Hoosick Falls is known throughout the whole country for its thriving manufacturing enterprises, and in this regard it must surely increase. And why? Simply because of the vast unused water-power at command and the determination of the leading citizens of the village to have this power utilized. Hoosick Falls is awake to its needs, and there is no reason why it should not make giant strides forward within the next few years.

The first manufacturing establishment in Hoosick Falls was about the year 1784, when Joseph Dorr leased a large area of land, together with the water-power on the north side of the river, and erected a carding and fulling-mill. Subsequently a flax-mill, a distillery and a saw-mill were erected upon this property. In 1786 Benjamin Colvin built a grist-mill on the south side of the river. In 1823 Joseph Gordon, a Scotchman, built what was known as the Caledonian cotton factory on the south bank of the Hoosick, and gave employment to about 150 persons. In 1831 two gentlemen named Benedict built the Tremont cotton factory on the north side of the river. In 1855 the Tremont factory property was sold to Walter A. Wood, and in 1869 the Caledonian factory was purchased by the Walter A. Wood Mowing and Reaping Machine Co., which now owns the entire power furnished by the cataract known as Hoosick falls. As everything pertaining to existing manufactures in Hoosick Falls is of interest, we append brief pen sketches of the various industrial enterprises.

WALTER A. WOOD MOWING AND REAPING MACHINE COMPANY.

The history of the extensive Walter A. Wood Reaper Works centers on the efforts and character of Mr. Wood himself, and may well arouse the ambition of young men originally dependent, like him, on their own unaided efforts. The founder and head of the business, Walter A. Wood, was a youth of great vigor of body and mind and boundless courage ; and these characteristics were regulated by common sense, a kindly disposition, and a deep respect for truth and honesty. He was born in Mason, Hillsboro County, N. H. By the time he had

WALTER A. WOODS MOWING AND REAPING MACHINE Co
THE LARGEST
IN THE WORLD

Residence of W. M. Holmes.

Residence of W. S. Nichols.

attained manhood he had mastered the trade of machinist, came to Hoosick Falls and worked in a machine shop, at once showing unusual skill and care in machine work and blacksmithing. After a time he became connected with the manufacture of agricultural implements, including plows; but seeing the possibilities of the then undeveloped reaper business he soon concentrated his attention on the making of harvest machinery. About the year 1850 he purchased a territorial right to make and sell the reaper known as the "John P. Manny," and opened the manufacture of it at Hoosick Falls, with improvements in its construction.

In 1855 he added to his facilities by buying the premises of the Tremont cotton factory.

In 1859 growing business compelled him to further extend his premises by renting a place formerly occupied by a competitor.

In November, 1860, his entire plant was practically annihilated by fire. The sales had averaged five thousand machines for two years previous. The same year the work of re-building began, and the factory was re-established with improved facilities. The Wood mower had already been added to his manufactures, and has remained a specialty ever since. It made a great success from the start.

In 1861 Walter A. Wood patented his "chain-rake reaper," a machine so unique and different from anything ever before conceived that perhaps no one ever looked upon it for the first time without being startled.

Wood's reapers and mowers had by this time acquired wide fame and his business was not only attracting attention from farmers, but from financial people in the business world. It now became no difficult matter to enlist larger capital, and in 1865 a number of gentlemen united in the formation of the Walter A. Wood Mowing and Reaping Machine Co., making him the president and superintendent.

The Wood establishment met with a second interruption by fire in 1870, but the check was in part neutralized by the lately acquired ownership of the Caledonia mill buildings which furnished a workshop while the burned premises were rebuilding. From the date of the 1870 fire new buildings have been year by year added to meet the heavy growth of business. It is difficult to show them in a picture owing to the separation of them by steep elevations of land in the plain which they occupy, but some idea may be gained by the picture printed in this publication.

In 1873 the reel-rake reaper known as the "Walter A. Wood sweep-rake reaper" was put forth with great success.

In 1874 the most striking enterprise in Mr. Wood's career up to the present time occurred in the introduction of the harvesting machine, which not only reaped the grain and separated it into gavels, but bound it into sheaves ready for the shock or stack.

In 1878 was introduced Wood's enclosed-gear mower, which was at once adopted as a type by European manufacturers.

In 1880 the company brought out their twine-binder harvester, to which was added Wood's bundle carrier, which deposited the sheaves in groups.

Novelties are still being brought out almost every year, and the production of the works was greater last season than ever before, being 82,970 machines—an average of 330 for each working day. In the numerous departments comprising the works upwards of 2000 men are employed.

The consumption of material for the season of 1890 included such items as the following: Steel and iron, 24,000 tons; coal, 8000 tons; grindstones, 220 tons; paints, 250 tons; rivets, 60 tons; brass, 60 tons; lubricating oils, 10,000 gallons; bolts, 5,000,000. In 1890 binding twine for harvesters was supplied to farmers to the amount of over 2500 tons.

The works stand on a tract of eighty-five acres of land on the west bank of the Hoosick River in a great bend of its course. They consist of the departments for blacksmith work, machinist work, wood-working, setting-up, painting, pattern shops, tool-making, grinding rooms, iron foundry, brass foundry, tumbling-barrel room, in and out freight depots, sample rooms, warehouses, boiler and engine houses, water-power buildings, a special fire-proof building for storing patterns, an inventions department, and a large and finely-fitted office building. In addition to the above departments the company has its own malleable iron works, constituting one of the best plants in existence. The large buildings throughout the premises are divided into sections by fire-proof walls extending several feet above the roofs. On a high point of land in the midst of the company's tract stands a large reservoir considerably higher than the roofs of the factory buildings and connected by pipes with all parts of the premises, with automatic sprinklers fastened to the ceilings. There is, also, independent fire apparatus housed in the yards, and there are hydrants and reels of hose provided in case of need.

All parts of the works are connected by private railroad tracks, which comprise seven miles on the grounds, with a full outfit of freight cars and two locomotives for switching cars to the public railroad, and moving materials and machines on the premises. Whole freight trains are quickly loaded at the company's freight houses and hauled by the company's locomotives to the track of the Fitchburg Railroad known as the "Hoosac Tunnel Line," thus bringing the works into prompt communication with all parts of the world.

The shops are lighted by electricity by the company's private plant, and the various departments are steam heated.

The river furnishes a fine water-power, the steam engines of the company being used merely as accessory power or in case of emergency. From the wood-working departments the sawdust is sucked into pipes which convey it to the boiler houses where it is utilized as fuel in making steam.

This great hive of industry ensconsed so favorably among the wholesome hills of the Hoosac region of east-

PLANT OF THE HOOSICK FALLS WATER POWER AND LIGHT CO.

ern New York has sent forth inventions which have received the highest prizes at all the World's Fairs ever held, and have made the names "Walter A. Wood" and "Hoosick Falls" familiar and famous in every country.

Up to the end of the 1890 season 875,369 Walter A. Wood machines had already been made, sent out and sold. And more than one-half of this immense number have been manufactured during the past nine years.

HOOSICK FALLS HOSIERY COMPANY.

This concern began operations in 1886, and was re-organized in 1889. The mill is what is known as a three-set mill, and gives employment to eighty persons, the pay-roll amounting to $2500 per month. The product is merino and all-wool underwear. This mill is operated by a syndicate which controls other knitting-mills. The product is sold through commission houses.

STEVENS & THOMPSON PAPER MILLS.

The industry conducted by the above firm is located on the Walloomsac River, at North Hoosick. The enterprise was established about thirty-five years ago; and it has been under the present management for twenty-one years. The individual members of the firm are S. S. Stevens, Geo. S. Thompson and F. L. Stevens. The head of the firm, who is the inventor of several appliances of vast interest to paper makers, has been connected with this industry since its inception. The mill produces specialties in wallpapers, its product being seven tons per day.

The Walloomsac Paper Co., whose mill is located at the village of Walloomsac, is composed of S. S. Stevens, Geo. S. Thompson, R. H. Thompson and F. L. Stevens. The product is sixteen tons of hanging paper daily.

Both of these mills are provided with the most approved machinery, are lighted with electric lights, and are run to their fullest capacity. The sales of product are chiefly in New York and Philadelphia. The two mills give employment to 100 persons.

HOOSICK FALLS CUSTOM MILLS.

Hurd & Co., the enterprising dealers in a variety of articles, referred to elsewhere, are proprietors of this industry, which is the only grist-mill in the village. and which is also the largest grain-handling concern between Troy and North Adams. The mill is a large wood and brick structure, built in 1878 by Chas. Q. Eldredge, and enlarged in 1880. It has two run of stone, with a capacity for grinding 350 bushels of corn and 100 bushels of wheat every ten hours. In the same building is an extensive wood-working establishment, fitted with all desirable machinery for dressing lumber, for planing, matching, scroll sawing, for manufacturing moldings and the various articles of house-finish produced by wood-working establishments. Over the establishment is a large shirt factory, which takes power from Hurd & Co.

Hurd & Co. are also manufacturers of chair stock in Hoosick Falls, while at Sandgate, Vt., the firm have a shingle-mill, and own an extensive tract of timber land.

SHIRT FACTORY.

A branch of the firm of Miller, Hall & Hartwell, shirt manufacturers, of Troy, occupies two floors 35x100 feet over Hurd & Co.'s wood-working shop. The firm was induced to locate here by Chas. Q. Eldredge, who erected the building, and its success here is shown in a constantly increasing business. The firm employs about 140 persons, produces 40,000 dozen shirts annually, and pays out $40,-000 per year for help alone.

HILAND CARPENTER.

Mr. Carpenter is located at North Hoosick, where he conducts a shirt manufactory and a plaster-mill. Mr. Carpenter has a large surplus water-power and property upon which a factory can be built.

LIVE BUSINESS MEN.

Hoosick Falls has a large number of "Eli" business men who "get there" with great force when matters of public importance are involved. Most of these men will be found represented in the apppendix to this publication by advertising cards. These advertisers have made it possible for the Board of Trade to issue this publication. Their contributions have aided materially in securing the work, and in spreading the excellent advantages possessed by Hoosick Falls as a location for industrial enterprise.

PARSONS' BAZAR.

This is the most extensive mercantile establishment in Hoosick Falls. It was established in 1849 by A. C. Parsons, and has been since 1853 at its present location, on Main Street. In 1868 Warren G. Parsons entered the house and the firm became A. C. Parsons & Son. Upon the death of the senior proprietor Warren succeeded to the business. The premises embrace four floors, 32x80 feet, with an elevator running from cellar to garret. The basement is used for reception and storage of goods, and has a track and car running the entire length. The first floor proper and second floor are used for display purposes, and the top story for storage. The business is dealing in shelf hardware, fine trimmings for builders' use, carpenters' and machinists' tools, hand agricultural implements, house-furnishing goods of all kinds, silverware, crockery, toys, guns, ammunition and fishing tackle, books, toilet cases, fine plush goods, papeteries, albums, pictures, text books, fine gift books, Christmas and birthday cards, etc. The stock in each department is as large as that carried in stores devoted to single lines.

CHAS. O. ELDREDGE.

Chas. O. Eldredge, the Secretary of the Board of Trade, is *the* real estate dealer of Hoosick Falls, where he has been a resident since 1873. He was for several years in the business at present conducted by Hurd & Co., is the second largest tax-payer in the village, and is a thorough "hustler" in all business matters. He built the Hoosick Falls Custom Mills, and secured the location here of a large shirt factory. He is prominently identified with the First National Bank, and it was chiefly to his efforts that the institution was started. His office, on Church Street, is the finest in town; it is heated by steam and lighted by a private electric plant, owned by himself. Mr. Eldredge is one of the village trustees, and believes in a brilliant future for Hoosick Falls. As to what he does and will do we call attention to his advertisement in appendix.

HAUSSLER & SON.

This concern is the oldest furniture and undertaking establishment in Hoosick Falls. It was established in 1859, and occupies commodious quarters in Wood's Block, Classic Street. Everything in the line of furniture of various grades, upholstery goods, pictures and frames, art goods and decorations are carried in stock, while a specialty is made of undertaking and embalming.

GILLESPIE BROS.

This firm began business in a small way, on John Street, in 1881, as the only strictly dry goods house in Hoosick Falls. In 1883 the concern moved into its present fine quarters, in Cheney Block, Main Street. Gillespie Bros. deal in dry goods, carpets and cloaks, and are leaders in their lines in town. The store is fitted with all modern improvements, including cash carriers, etc. The individual members of the firm are Chester Gillespie and Nelson Gillespie, whose lives have been devoted to dry goods

Holmes Block, Classic Street.

Residence of J. Hobart Warren.

Cheney Block, Main and Classic Streets.

Residence of Hon. J. Russell Parsons.

business. They occupy two floors of a double store, employ ten persons, and their trade extends to all parts of the surrounding country, while as a progressive firm they are known all over the State.

EASTON, RISING & WORDEN.

In 1875 Mr. C. W. Easton opened a general insurance and coal business in Hoosick Falls, attaining considerable success. In 1880 he formed a partnership with Mr. C. F. Rising, and in 1883 Messrs. Easton & Rising took a third partner in the person of Mr. L. E. Worden, when the present firm was established. The firm are contractors and builders, and dealers in builders' supplies, lumber, doors, sash, blinds, builders' hardware, lime, cement, paints and oils, agricultural implements, etc. The firm also represent some of the largest insurance companies; and do a large business in each line represented.

ROCHESTER CLOTHING COMPANY.

This wide-a-wake concern is located in Byars Block, Church Street, and occupies a handsome double store. The business was started in May, 1890, and is the largest of its class in town. The house deals in everything in the way of men's, youths' and boys' clothing, hats, furnishing goods, etc., the clothing being of the reliable Rochester make. The store is conducted by a syndicate which operates a number of stores throughout the country, supplying the same with goods of their own manufacture. Mr. Edward Levy is manager of the house here.

S. S. LOTTRIDGE.

This establishment has a history extending over a period of half a century. The concern deals in carpenters' and builders' supplies of all kinds, both wood and metal, plastering material, marble for walks, drain tile, and a great variety of specialties; also manufactures buggies, carriages and cutters. The firm owns a large amount of real estate in convenient localities. A specialty is made of contracting and building, and in this regard the house partakes of the character of a building and loan association, as it builds homes for people of small means, and grants long terms of payment.

SALEM H. WHITE.

Mr. White occupies commodious quarters in his own building, corner First and Centre Streets, and deals in meats, poultry and vegetables. He has been in business about four years, is a young man, and has built up a large business.

H. P. BERGER & CO.

This firm occupy roomy quarters extending to four floors, in the handsome Holmes Block, Classic Street. The business is dealing in furniture of all grades, pianos and organs, pictures and frames, drapery, rugs, and in the manufacture of cabinet work. The firm began business in October, 1890. The individual members are H. P. Berger and W. M. Holmes. Mr. Holmes, who is president of the Board of Trade and a village trustee, is the owner of the building, and the inventor of a twine-binder manufactured by the Wood Mowing & Reaping Machine Co. The store is finely fitted and is supplied with all conveniences for conducting a large business.

JOSEPH BUCKLEY.

Mr. Buckley is a dealer in groceries and provisions, coal, wood and ice. He makes a specialty of D. & H. C. Co.'s and D., L. & W. R. R. Co.'s rail coal, and promptly attends to all orders. Mr. Buckley started business in a small way about fifteen years ago at his present location, opposite Troy & Boston passenger depot, and has built up a very large business through his own efforts. The fact that he has been president of the village and is now first vice-president of the Board of Trade indicates the esteem in which he is held among his neighbors.

E. LEONARD & SON.

This concern was established in 1852 by Mr. E. Leonard, who admitted his son, Edgar, into partnership upon his reaching manhood. Upon the death of the senior proprietor Edgar became sole proprietor and retained the old firm name. Leonard & Son are agents of the National Express Co., expressmen, ice dealers, and run a number of job wagons. They do a carrying business of all kinds of merchandise, baggage, etc., and give special attention to moving pianos.

HURD & CO.

The business of this house was established in 1866. It has been under the administration of the present firm since 1887. The firm are proprietors of the Hoosick Falls Custom Mills and other industries referred to under the head of manufactures. At No. 5 Center Street is the office and store of the house. Hurd & Co. are wholesale and retail dealers in wood and lumber, agricultural implements, doors, sash and blinds, drain tile, roofing slate, builders' hardware and supplies. They do a large business as contractors and builders, also, and form one of the largest concerns in the place.

BRIEN BROS.

This firm began business about two years ago, and has been located in the new Holmes Block since April last. In addition to their quarters here the firm have a storehouse on Church Street. The individual members of the firm are F. S., L. J., and J. T. Brien, while two other brothers and seven other men are employed about the establishment, making a working force of twelve. Brien Bros. deal in heavy and shelf hardware, tools, stoves, ranges and furnaces. This is the only firm in Hoosick Falls that buys stoves in carload lots. The firm does plumbing, gas and steam fitting, roofing and general job work, and its facilities are such that it is enabled to contract for jobs of any magnitude in steam heating, water piping, etc., in any part of the country.

McEACHRON & ROBSON.

This house has a history dating 1849. It has been under the administration of the present proprietors since 1887. Its location is on John Street, where it enjoys nicely fitted and roomy quarters. The individual members of the firm are J. H. McEachron and C. A. Robson. The house deals in and has a large stock of fine diamonds and jewelry, watches, clocks, silverware, musical instruments and optical goods, makes a specialty of fitting glasses and of difficult repairing.

RILEY & GAFFNEY.

This well-known firm conduct a large livery, sale and boarding stable, and deal in harness, buggies and carriages, and in coal, wood and sand. They make a specialty of fine matched pairs and single horses, and have an extended reputation as reliable dealers in horses. The individnal members of the firm are Frank Riley and Peter Gaffney. The establishment has been in existence for twenty years, and for the past year and a-half under its present management. Mr. Riley, of the firm, is president of the village and second vice-president of the Board of Trade.

COMMERCIAL HOUSE.

The Commercial House is a large brick structure, located opposite the railroad depot. It is heated by steam, lighted by electricity, its rooms are comfortable and well furnished, its table substantial and bounteous, and the general character of the house home-like. The proprietor, Mr. Frederick Deming, has had a long experience in hotel business, and meets the demands of guests.

ON THE HOOSICK RIVER

J. H. GLENN.

Mr. Glenn's cosy store is located at the corner of First and Centre Streets. He has been in business about two years, deals in groceries and provisions, fruits and vegetables, and is in possession of a prosperous business.

HENRY W. STONE.

Mr. Stone is located at No. 8 John Street, where he has been in business about six years. He is a druggist and apothecary, and, in addition to a full line of drugs and chemicals, he is agent for Boericke & Tafel's and Humphrey's Homeopathic remedies, Penfield's celluloid trusses, and Henderson's bulk garden seeds.

CORNELIUS McCAFFERY.

Mr. McCaffery's office is on Third Street. About twelve years ago he opened a blue stone quarry which has since furnished stone for many buildings in Hoosick Falls. The stone, which dresses nicely, can be furnished in any size block desired. The quarry is easily accessible, and convenient for shipping to any point.

EDWIN H. MAXON.

Mr. Maxon is a photographer, who made the negatives from which the engravings presented in this publication were produced. He is a true artist, as is evinced by the character of his photographs. He is located at Estabrook Gallery, Main Street, and makes a specialty of children's pictures.

W. M. ARCHIBALD.

Mr. Archibald conducts the oldest drug store in town, at No. 21 Classic Street. He has been in business for fourteen years, and deals in a general line of drugs, chemicals, etc., in addition to which he manufactures Archibald's Rheumatic Cure and Archibald's Quinsy Cure. These remedies are very efficacious, are well recommended, and enjoy a good sale.

P. M. YOULEN.

Mr. Youlen is a watchmaker and jeweler, doing business on Main Street, head of John. He has been in business in Hoosick Falls nearly eight years. Mr. Youlen deals in watches, clocks, jewelry and optical goods, and makes a specialty of fine repairing.

DAVID DARLING.

Mr. Darling is a contractor and builder, who constructs public buildings, stores and dwellings complete, furnishes plans, drawings, etc. His responsibility is unquestioned, and his promptness is testified to by twenty-five years' experience.

WM. SHERIDAN.

Mr. Sheridan is the proprietor of the Hoosick House, 32 Main Street, and is a dealer in ales, wines, liquors and cigars. He is a clear-headed gentleman, who held the office of overseer of the poor for two years, and is at present one of the trustees of the village.

CHAS. LASOR.

Mr. Lasor is a painter, grainer and paper hanger, and is in possession of a nice business. He is also manager of Wood's Opera House, and is city bill poster.

E. R. ESTABROOK.

Mr. Estabrook has lived in Hoosick Falls for a long period, and is the oldest insurance agent in the place. He represents a number of strong companies, and places insurance to any amount, while his long career has given him the confidence of the public.

JOHN GALLAGHER.

Mr. Gallagher has been engaged in coal business in Hoosick Falls for about ten years. He deals in all kinds of coal, making a specialty of D. & H. C. Co.'s rail coal. His yard is on Railroad Avenue. Mr. Gallagher attends to all orders promptly.

CONSTITUTION

OF THE

BOARD OF TRADE

OF

HOOSICK FALLS

ADOPTED OCTOBER 21, 1890.

SECTION I.—NAME.

This Association shall be called the Board of Trade of the Village of Hoosick Falls.

SECTION II.—OBJECT.

Its object shall be to aid in promoting the extension and development of the industrial and other interests of the village.

SECTION III.—OFFICERS.

The officers of this Association shall be a President, two Vice-Presidents, a Secretary and a Treasurer.

The officers shall be elected separately, by ballot, at the regular annual meeting of the Board, and shall hold their respective offices for the period of one year, beginning on the first day of January after their election, and until their successors shall be duly chosen. *Provided*, that the persons first chosen to fill said offices shall respectively hold the same from the date of their election until the first day of January, A. D. 1891.

President.

It shall be the duty of the President to preside at all meetings of the Board, and he shall be (*ex-officio*) a member of all standing committees of the Board.

In the absence of the President the Vice-President, First or Second, shall perform his duties.

Secretary.

The Secretary shall keep minutes of the proceedings of the Board, and discharge such other duties as the Board may prescribe.

Treasurer.

It shall be the duty of the Treasurer, after his election and before entering upon the discharge of his duties, to file a bond for the faithful performance of the same in an amount satisfactory to the Executive Committee. He shall then, as Treasurer, take charge of all moneys accruing to the Association; he shall pay out moneys on warrants drawn by the President and countersigned by the Secretary; he shall keep a regular account of the moneys received and expended by him, and shall make an annual report thereof, and such other reports as the Executive Committee may require.

SECTION IV.—COMMITTEES.

The President shall, as soon as practicable, and within one week after his election, appoint the following committees, to hold offices for the term of one year from and after the first day of January succeeding their appointment, provided that the committees appointed by the first President of the Board shall hold office from the date of their appointment until the first day of January, A. D. 1891.

Membership.

A Committee on Membership, to consist of three members, whose duty it shall be to receive and report upon all applications for membership.

Finance.

A Committee on Finance, to consist of three members, whose duty it shall be to audit all bills before payment, and to audit the general accounts of the Treasurer, and to have general charge and supervision of the finances of the Board.

Trade and Manufacture.

A Committee on Trade and Manufacture, to consist of five members, whose duty it shall be to promote the manufacturing and business interests of the village; to receive and investigate all applications looking to the establishment of new industries in the village, and to report their action thereon, or any recommendation they may see fit to make concerning the same, to the Board.

Public Works.

A Committee on Public Works, to consist of three members, whose duty it shall be to aid in securing public buildings for Hoosick Falls, to look after the interest of the village in relation to its railroads, depots, hotels, water works, mail and telegraph service, and suggest improvements to same.

Statistics.

A Committee on Statistics, to consist of three members, whose duties shall be to procure all information possible in relation to comparative freight rates between this and other inland villages, to closely watch taxation and how the same compares with neighboring villages, to also watch census and other reports going out from the village, and to see that the same are correctly issued, to scan carefully all figures and statements that appear in print in relation to our village, and when thought necessary to call attention of Board to same.

Executive.

An Executive Committee, consisting of the officers of the Board and chairmen of their various committees, who shall have general supervision of the business interests of the Association, and shall prepare and have charge of all publications and printing.

SECTION V.—MEMBERSHIP AND DUES.

All citizens of the village of Hoosick Falls who shall declare their intention to become members of the Board to the Secretary of the Board prior to January 1st, 1891, shall be charter members.

Any resident of the village of Hoosick Falls may be proposed for membership in writing to the Committee on Membership, and upon a favorable report by said committee the names of persons so reported shall be balloted upon at any regular meeting of the Board, and any of said persons receiving a two-thirds vote of the members present shall become a member of the Board.

On becoming a member he shall sign the Constitution and By-Laws.

Dues.

Each member shall pay to the Treasurer, within thirty days after being admitted to membership, an admission fee of three dollars; and each member shall pay to the Treasurer annual dues of two dollars, payable semi-annually, on or before January 10th and July 10th in each and every year.

SECTION VI.—MEETINGS.

The annual meeting of the Board shall be held on the second Monday of December in each year.

Regular quarterly meetings shall be held on the second Monday of January, April, July and October. Special meetings may be called at any time by the President, or in his absence by either of the Vice-Presidents.

The Secretary shall send a written or printed notice of all meetings to each member, by mail, at least three days before such meeting.

SECTION VII.

This Constitution may be altered or amended by a vote of two-thirds of the members of the Association present at any regular meeting, provided a written notice of such amendment shall have been given at a previous meeting.

BY-LAWS.

CHAPTER I.

Meetings.

Rule 1. At Business meetings of the Board of Trade members shall sit uncovered, and preserve a proper decorum. Any member wishing to speak will rise and address the chair.

Rule 2. No member may speak longer than five minutes, nor more than twice on the same motion, unless by consent of the Board of Trade.

Rule 3. No debate shall be permitted except to a motion regularly made and seconded. At the request of any member motions shall be reduced to writing by the mover thereof.

Rule 4. At the regular meetings of the Board the following shall be the order of business, and this order shall not be waived without unanimous consent, viz.:

1. Call to order.
2. Roll call.
3. Reading of minutes.
4. Reading of communications.

5. Reports of Standing Committees, as follows: On Membership; on Finance; on Trade and Manufactures; on Public Works; on Statistics.
6. Reports from Secretary.
7. Reports from Special Committees.
8. Unfinished business.
9. New business.
10. Adjournment.

CHAPTER II.

Quorum.

Rule 1. Ten members thereof shall constitute a quorum at meetings of the Board of Trade.

CHAPTER III.

Committees.

Rule 1. The Committee on Public Works shall consider matters relating to the mail service, telegraphs and telephones, public buildings, railroads, water supply, sanitary measures, streets, roads, bridges, and such other kindred matters as may be referred to them by the Board.

Rule 2. The Committee on Trade and Manufacture shall consider questions relating to the introduction, fostering and encouragement of manufacturing industries in Hoosick Falls and its suburbs.

CHAPTER IV.

Withdrawal of Membership.

Any member who may wish to withdraw from the Association shall give written notice thereof, but shall not be permitted to withdraw unless he shall have paid his dues.

CHAPTER V.

Expulsion of Members.

Any member who shall refuse or neglect to comply with the Constitution and By-Laws of the Association may be expelled by the vote of three-fourths of the members present; but a notice of said motion shall be served on him by the Secretary previous to the day of said meeting.

Any member refusing to pay his dues shall have two monthly notices served upon him by the Secretary, informing him of the fact; and his refusal to pay after being so notified shall cause his name to be stricken from the roll of membership.

CHAPTER VI.

Amendments.

Rule 1. These rules may be amended, or additional ones adopted, by unanimous consent at any regular meeting, without previous notice, or by an affirmative vote of two-thirds of the members present at a regular meeting, if notice of the same has been given at the preceding regular meeting, or published twice in a newspaper in Hoosick Falls, for two weeks prior to the meeting at which they are acted upon.

Appendix.

www.ingramcontent.com/pod-product-compliance
Lightning Source LLC
Chambersburg PA
CBHW021628270326
41931CB00008B/918

* 9 7 8 3 3 3 7 1 9 3 4 5 4 *